THE FIRST INHABITANTS OF ARCADIA

The First Inhabitants
of Arcadia

Poems by
Christopher Bursk

The University of Arkansas Press
Fayetteville
2006

Copyright © 2006 by The University of Arkansas Press
ISBN-10   1-55728-813-5
ISBN-13   978-1-55728-813-4

10   09   08   07   06   5   4   3   2   1

Designed by Liz Lester

LIBRARY OF CONGRESS
CATALOGING-IN-PUBLICATION DATA

Bursk, Christopher.
The first inhabitants of Arcadia : poems /
by Christopher Bursk.
p.   cm.
ISBN 1-55728-813-5 (pbk. : alk. paper)
I. Title.
PS3552.U765F57   2006
811'.54—dc22
2005029967

ACKNOWLEDGMENTS

This manuscript owes a debt of gratitude to Luray Gross, Steven Huff, Betsy Sholl, Pam and Herb Perkins-Frederick, Helen Lawton Wilson, George Drew, Baron Wormser, and Richard Jackson and the Vermont Post-graduate Writers' Conference Manuscript Workshop.

The author is especially grateful to Enid Shomer—for her editing and for her poetry, and to Rona Cohen for her wise counsel.

Poems from the manuscript appeared in *Bucks County Writer* ("The Burden of Being the First Letter," "'The business of a poet,'" "Dictionary Johnson," and "Boycott Lettuce! Boycott Grapes!"); *The Sun* ("What's Worth Keeping"); and *Dogwood Journal* ("Count to a Thousand before You Open the Door" and "Insufficient, Incompetent, Incapable").

The author is indebted to John Wain's *Samuel Johnson: A Biography* (New York: Viking Press, 1974) and Professor Winslow of Boston University, illustrious go-betweens for the great doctor and a young graduate student. Passages from *Dr. Johnson's Dictionary* are drawn from the remarkable Levenger Press edition (Delray Beach, 2002) edited by Jack Lynch.

"Working the Stacks" was the title poem of a chapbook from Bacchae Press and is reprinted with the gracious permission of that press.

CONTENTS

⌒ 3 ⌒

THE FIRST INHABITANTS OF ARCADIA

❧ I ❧

To deliberate whenever I doubted, to enquire whenever I was ignorant, would have protracted the undertaking without end, and, perhaps, without much improvement. . . . I saw that one enquiry only gave occasion to another, that book referred to book, that to search was not always to find, and to find was not always to be informed; and thus to pursue perfection was, like the first inhabitants of Arcadia, to chace the sun, which, when they had reached the hill where he seemed to rest, was still beheld at the same distance from them.

—SAMUEL JOHNSON,
"PREFACE TO THE DICTIONARY"

Learning to Read

For Elizabeth Raby

By four I knew what my mother must have known
immediately. I was more trouble
than I was worth. She'd lie down for her nap and there I'd be
buzzing about her, thinking
that I had a right to push my nose into everything.
That's how I learned: bumping into things
like a fly that keeps asking the same question
of glass. At seven I hovered over words
on cereal boxes, candy wrappers,
my grandmother's romance novels, my brother's
adventure books. They all tasted
like delicacies, like the crust
of fat off the roast, dollop
of butter, heel of bread, smear of gooseberry jam,
sweet, brown rot
of a banana, still-soft gum with a little peppermint
hidden in it. I was that hungry.
Leftovers, scraps, carrion. As I turned the pages,
I picked my nose, studied scabs,
the blue grit I pried from under my nails,
the bit of wax on my fingertip,
reading the smudged ink
of my body, its own dark alphabet.
I didn't care what I feasted on
as long as I feasted.

Don't Move

Don't even think of moving.
His mother has dragged him by the ear
to the chair. *Do you think that I'm stupid?*
Do you imagine that I won't know
if you've budged, even one inch,
from this spot? His mother pulls the door shut,
so the click of the lock is her last word. Gone.
She'll be out all afternoon. The boy could get up,
look into any drawer, eat whatever he wanted
that was bad for him, open the window,
drop to the ground and walk away.
Instead he sits on his hands and rocks
from side to side. First his body is light
on his right hand
and the left falls under the accusing pressure
of a sudden weight. Then it's the left
shown a little pity, the right pressed down
flat to the bone. He's conducting an experiment
to see how much pain
he can take. Each finger bone gets its turn
to ache and protest.
If his mother wants him to stay in one place,
then he will. He'll follow her orders
to the letter, sit here till his body can take no more
even if it means soiling himself.
He'll teach his mother a lesson
about language. *What are you doing*

in that chair? she asks when she opens the door.
It's beautiful outside. That's what parents do:
they make a habit of forgetting
the very words meant
to be remembered. When his mother sees
the darkened pants leg, the little puddle
on the chair he's still
sitting in, she makes him stand,
loosens his belt. His trousers drop to the floor.
Oh my poor boy, what am I to do with you?

More Investigations
into the Nature of Language

You still can't get over your good fortune:
to be old enough to be allowed blades
this sharp, this sure
of themselves. Real scissors, one of the privileges
of being sick. You move the metal around the bosom
of a woman wearing nothing
but a bra and panties so lacy it's like cutting a snowflake.
You clip a man in a smoking jacket
out of his dark upholstered den.
Easy as choosing a raindrop
and cutting it free
from a storm, you snip a girl
out of her gym glass, pluck a boy from his hive
of friends. Twins sheared from a swing set.
A woman in a gown so long
it lets the floor know what elegance is.
A pilot carved out of his cockpit.
A power forward released from the rim of the hoop.
A grandmother detached from her apron.
By afternoon's end you have a whole town of half-dressed
men unbuckled from their cars,
women unbuttoned from their homes,
throats and shoulders, thighs and legs cut clear of the thicket
of the actual, unhinged from
the obligations of place and time.

Could your father say as much?
You don't ask him this
as he comes in the door. You look up
from the girls you've cleaved from their families,
boys separated even from the rule of gravity,
and detect in your father's face what? Regret?
Amazement? Shame? There are no words
in the language for what you see
in his face and what he sees in yours.
You both do what sons and fathers do: turn back
to your work.

The Ars Poetica of Baseball Cards

In fifth grade I fell in love with the tired, capable bodies
of second basemen already old
by thirty, utility infielders just one bad hop away
from being released; .237 hitters
who'd stare down relievers the way someone might stand in a highway
and dare trucks to hit them; Peanuts Lowrey,
Luke Easter, Chico Carasquel, Dusty Rhodes.
By the fourth grade I'd learned to love the abstract
justice of names: Billy Consolo, Ted Lepcio,
the o bouncing at the end of their names
like a ball scooped out of the dirt between second and third,
and the catchers, Andy Seminick, Mickey Owen, Smokey Burgess,
Yogi Berra, men built, it seems,
to squat down. I could see the fastball, high inside,
concealed in the glove
of Mel Parnell, a man born to play with the Red Sox
the way some men are destined
to be shipwrecked. As soon as his dad named him,
Hoyt Wilhelm had to throw a knuckleball.
Warren Spahn, Junior Gilliam, Nellie Fox—
where else could I hold a man in my hands
and look into his eyes without him
turning away. I was as free to gaze at him
as I was to gaze into water.
Eddie Waitkus, Jimmy Piersall, Ed Bouchee,
lifted free of the messy exigencies of their lives,
the Mexican Leagues, Korea, a shooting, a breakdown,

a man's entire year measured in at-bats, singles, doubles, homeruns, rbi's,
and each man smelled of bubble gum, pink, sweet,
hard gum I'd chew
until the taste was gone and then I'd chew some more
out of pure loyalty. I still know Milt Bolling's weight
in 1954 (178), the color of Billy Klaus's eyes
(hazel). Sacrifice fly, squeeze play,
southpaws, Texas Leaguers, pinch runners—
I grew more and more indebted
to language, the tiny print at the back
of the Topps cards, the stories they told
in only a few words, those old journeymen
who'd fill in at any position, play not spectacularly
but just good enough to keep the game
within reach, veterans who stared off into the distance
because they'd heard what no one else had,
a door closing, a train pulling out.

Servants

For Luray Gross

My mother gone for months, my brothers away at school,
I'd open the dictionary and there were:
Dishabille, the French governess, or *Scurrilous,* the riding master,

Worry always at her needle, or *Corpulent,* the cook,
all so much more interesting
than the kids at school or my father's weekend cronies.

They even smelled better
and the smells had stories to tell:
Nutmeg, Hedge Garlic, Turmeric, Clove.

They just needed a little prompting.
I liked to imagine words putting up their feet by the fire
and talking of their masters,

stiff-backed *Faithful,* snail-faced *Obedient,*
mousy *Useful,* usually discreet *Wisdom*
siphoning off a little of their lord's best brandy

and telling a few off-color jokes,
even footmen and chambermaids deserving a life.
Misery, Rancor, Mischief, Solitude, over-worked, under-

paid help that had done their best
to raise me. So what if I couldn't open my mouth
at school? So what if I had trouble talking

to my father? I was included in the ribald
secret life of vowels and consonants,
Raillery, Rumor, Escapade,

my nanny, my scullery maid, my gamekeeper,
their belly laughs in the stables,
winks in the parlor, their carryings-on beneath the stairs.

Multiple Personality Disorder

Time? In junior high I had so much
                    on my hands
          I invented
theories about the letters
                    of the alphabet
         and the lives they led,
especially the ingenuity required
                    of a vowel, silent
         e, for example. It had no
choice but to adapt to every
                    sort of circumstance:
         one moment, the demure
domestic, able to endure any
                    indignity; the next
         a hunched-over magician with
power to transform *trip*
                    into *tripe, slop*
         into *slope, fat* into
fate, crap into *crape*. One more
                  of *e*'s sleight
         of hand tricks: Now it's a *shame*.
Now it's a *sham*. Tricky
                 e disguised as *y?*
         Determined *e* im-
personating *u?* Lowercase *e*
                    with its MPD, just part
         of a large family used to wearing

each other's clothes, bumping

                    into themselves,

          molecules

crammed into a too small room,

                    language

          not knowing what

else to do but talk

                    to itself. Long

          to short. Short to

silent.

F

F, one more letter that deserves a whole book devoted to it,
                                        the alphabet's Little Lord
Fauntelroy, flaunting its frills, its French cuffs, its fluency
                                        in foreign languages, flamboyant
fricative I fell for the way other boys fall for football players,
                                        infatuated with the
figure it cut, uppercase *F* I'd write over and over
                                        just to feel it
float over the page as some suitors might fill whole notebooks
                                        with their beloved's
full name—though I was even more fond of lowercase
                                        f, its ferocity,
fealty, the way it faced facts, let its faith be tested,
                                        how it refused to
flinch, the teeth biting the lower lip, the air
                                        forced out, that sigh that
finishes so many words, first part of so many oaths
                                        for God and country,
for chrissake, for pity's sake, forswearing all others,
                                        forsaking no one,
forever true, the perfect letter for a fourteen-year-old—though
                                        how's he going to admit
falling so in love with a consonant, he'd fain die
                                        for it, that flighty

fop of a letter, fatalist, finagler, freedom fighter, fancy pants,
                                    the way it
flounces, flicks its hips, stretches out its arms, flings itself
                              forward into the future.

Ode to *j*

just as often bouncing a little ball
                    off its nose,
            as about to e-
ject from its seat, it teaches the frogs to
                    jet-propel off
            their lily pads, the pond to
jitterbug, the rain to
                    appreciate its own
            jive, the storm to stop apolo-
gizing. By junior high I'd tired
                    of words, their bullying
            justifications, glittering
generalities. I'd forgotten
                    about the revelry
            certain letters enga-
ge in, their jujitsu, jam sessions, juicy
                    stories, the secret
            pleasures of jealousy
and bad jokes. How could I give up hope
                    in a world where
            j's the silent letter in mari-
juana? It jostles. It jars.
                    What's a kid to do
            but take all the

joy he can, light up a joint,
jack off,
jiggle the brain,
jolt the body? Juggler, jester,
renegade *i*,
the alphabet's adopted child,
j's got the tongue talking
to the roof of the mouth,
a new kind of
justice, something as common
as air
turned into
jubilation. The brain
has precious few
pleasures and *j*,
jocund, jaunty
j, is one of them.

Letter *l* as in
Reliable, Indomitable, Chivalrous

For Lorraine Lins

It's hard not to like
       l. Life.
   Love. Luck. It's so full
of lofty ideals. A natural born leader
      of all the laggard
   vowels, lugubrious *u,*
ever loitering *e,* loopy *o.*
        Think, *l* seems to say,
    of all you can accomplish
if you work as diligently
      as an adverb.
   It latches on
to an adjective and sweetly
      softly, almost indiscernibly,
   persuades it to
spread its goodwill to the rest
      of the sentence.
   Lambent. Luminous.
Lucent. What pleasure there is
      in working certain words
   into sentences. *L* changes
everything. Unflinching-
      ly, unstintingly, it labors,
   Let the earth

put forth vegetation, plants

                    yielding seed, and fruit trees
            fruit in which is their seed.
That's not just the Lord

                    talking. That's
            language. *Let there be . . .*
How lovely it feels

                    to tuck the tongue
            against the teeth
and let the lungs do the rest.

M-m-m Good!

Mummy. Mom. Mater. Mother.
Mutter. Madre.
It's no coincidence,
maybe, that the mammary glands
whose soft folds you push
your face into, whose
milk and melodies you first drink in,
begin with *m.*
Those mythic, magnetic
magnanimous, impossibly a-
musing, comfy, yum-
my, scrumptious breasts.
M's a letter you don't have to breathe
to say. The lips do
most of the work,
milking sound out of that prodigiously
mushy, remarkably un-
squeamish body part.
Monkeys. Magpies. Masturbation.
Mucous. Mutilation.
Murder. Mystery.
Martyrdom. The mind
makes whatever
music it can, moanings
mutterings, musings,
broken
measures.

Hearing the Word for the First Time

The *n* without scruples
kicking the legs out from under a kid,
the *i* caught up
in what it had no intentions of doing:
ganging up with the twins,
double *g*, those thugs up to no good
again.
The more I tried not to think it,
the more I couldn't
get it out of my mind. My eighth-grade teacher,
my swim coach,
every black person I bumped against in the street
must be able to read
my thoughts and see that I was no different
from everyone else.
Why were words invented
if we weren't supposed to
say them? Particular consonants
luring particular vowels
into all kinds of cruel pranks.
Hearing the word hurled at him,
how does a boy ever trust language
again, even well-intentioned *e*
and hard-working *r?*
I'd worked so hard
to keep my lips from forming the two syllables,
finally all I wanted to do

was say them and get it over with.
        Like being forbidden to
spit in public, till that's all
        you want to do.
Like being given a rock and told not to
        throw it; asked to pretend
it isn't even in your hand,
        but already grieving
the window broken
        without the stone
ever leaving your fist.

At An Early Age a Boy Discovers
the Pleasures and Perils of Double *o*

For Jo Sodano

Put these silly identical twins
            o and *o*
                in a word and it goes goofy,
but endearing. *Buffoon.*
                      Booby. Nincompoop.
            Your mother's not crazy
just a little loony. That's not shit
                in your pants
            but poopy.
Add one more *o* to *lose*
                and you're loose
            and ashamed
of nothing but ready
                for everything: *Cookie!*
          Snookie! Whoopie! Booze!
Floozies! Words only too willing
                to pooh-pooh
            the alphabet's great aspirations,
that silly goose. How far
                would you get with a girl
          if *seduce* were spelled
sedoos? What conclusions
                would a philosopher
          dedoos? What if

there were nothing loopy
                    in the language, no
          va-va voom? No magic
broom. No swooping wings?
                    No dark lagoon?
          No fingernail
moon? No freedom to ooh
                    and ahh, to swoon?
          Nothing too
gorgeous for words?
                    Too, small extremist,
          pipsqueak adverb, always
piping up, *Too much?*
                    There's never
          too much!

Why a Boy Is Drawn to Lowercase *p*

It even looks dirty, dangling
              below the line
     like a kid taking a leak
while treading water. For some boys
             that's paradise:
     to be able to piss
in public, an appealing puerility
             to lowercase *p—peepee*
     penis, prick, poop
and the ability to produce it,
             perhaps the closest
     a kid gets to the seat
of power. *Pontiff. Preacher. Professor.*
             Parent. Principal.
     Prime Minister.
Proctologist. What a bore
             to be anything that begins
     with capital letter *P.*
Put little upside down
             b, shepherd's crook,
     tiny periscope,
at the front of a word, and you've got
             a whole alphabet
of pickpockets and pimps,
defrocked priests, perverts,
             pinch hitters,
     pantywaists,

pipsqueaks—lowercase
                    p and its small platoon,
          faces with no eyes
or mouths, bodies with no arms
                    or legs; prodigious,
          precocious,
promiscuous language's
                    brilliant im-
          perfections.

Vocabulary Test

Discharged. Defunct. Dead. Deformed.
What better way to learn
to hate the language? To be graded for making words
nothing but what you're told they must
mean. Conscript them, good little soldiers
sent off to a war that they had no say in starting.
Daunted, Disheartened, Distraught,
I lined my words up till they formed a platoon
of disabled veterans
wounded decades before, *Disconsolate, Dispirited,*
defeated by battles they couldn't stop
talking about, one more depleted army
determined to march
to destruction. *Distress.*
Disappointment. What else had a boy
to look forward to? Still another report
on Pope's *The Rape of the Lock?*
The next hundred pages of *Silas Marner?*
One more mass-produced advanced placement essay
so I could go to college and major in Usefulness
and get a job like my dad's?
No, I'd pledge my allegiance to
discouragement. I'd turn
discontent into a career. I'd give myself to
despair. What more glorious a cause to die for
than *disenchantment,*

disillusionment,

despondency! It'd be like joining the French

Foreign Legion. *Dismay. Desperation.*

Depression. Dementia!

With comrades like these what had a lad to fear?

⌘♓□□♓♦⍓ □⬩♍♋□

For Teresa Mendez-Quigley

For that opening
I always looked for
in blind alleys,
for the paths only water could
find through stone,
for the way to lean like trees
bent in the wind
as they listened
to a music only they could hear.
If I'd been a resourceful
or brave child,
I'd have spoken
the language I used alone,
etched in frost
on windows
or left in the sugar spilled
on the table, a lexicon
for all the hurts, terrors, hungers
I couldn't account for,
written with the dew
of leaves and on the fog

of windshields, the air I stepped into,
                    the night sky.
            I wanted to talk
with the world. The whole,
                        impossibly
        huge world.

What a Boy Knows and Doesn't Know

The man's fingers had moved across you
taking little tucks
as if fitting you for a costume
or sewing a shadow to you—shoulders, arms, the small
of the back, inside of the leg. Weeks later
you could still feel the needle's
piercing, each stitch
pulled taut. Nothing in school
or in church or at home
had prepared you for something that intimate
next to your skin, an embroidery
you couldn't undo, even if you wished to.
You did not know the words
for what the man had tried to do
in the car. You had no name
to put to what fit so tightly now.
So you spoke to no one till you began to wonder
if you'd wanted it
to happen or even if it had
or could or would
again. And when you learned the language
for what you'd felt, you knew
what many boys know, but do not know
how to explain, their lives
ruled by what they do
with this knowledge or do not

do. You'd discovered your name
was not the only one
you'd been given, the road you'd taken
led to more places
than you'd expected, and other means of transportation.

Dictionary Johnson

House to market, church
to tavern, the man whose job it was to decide
what went into the dictionary
and what did not, counted the steps. He made sure
his foot touched a particular stone at a particular time,
and turned back if his fingers failed to brush a certain post
along the way. No walk
for the great man was ever simple. No floor
safe till he tried its strength,

no sentence. It helped to know
that someone I was studying in school,
a man who held himself responsible
for the entire English language,
was as screwed up as I was. At eighteen, in the midst
of decisions that I was convinced
would determine the rest of my life—whether or not
to quit the football team or smile
at a certain boy or girl or take Calculus I or Spanish IV—
it was comforting to think of Dr. Johnson

standing at the top of the hill of a great estate
and slowly removing from his pockets
keys, watch, purse,
and handing them all to the lord of the manor
and then lying in the grass
and rolling down, down, down

like a great boulder till he hit the bottom,
and then rising and with as much dignity
as when he'd greeted the king, going back up the slope
and flinging his body back down
as if there was real pleasure in doing certain things
over and over and it took a great man
to know what they were.

∽ 2 ∼

Thirty years after his father had asked him to watch the bookstall, his family's only livelihood, and Sam being seventeen, too in love with sneering, had refused, the author of arguably the greatest dictionary ever returned to his native village and in a downpour so heavy no one sensible even thought of going outside, and with no covering for his head, stood in the square on the exact site where his father's bookstall had been, and out of grief and penance, language's surest foundation, stared down the townsfolk's mockery, and let the rain teach him a lesson as only it could.

—WALTER R. RAWLINGS,
SAMUEL JOHNSON'S OTHER LIFE

Working the Stacks

For Patricia Goodrich

Reach up for the light cord and tug through its little knot
of resistance, and there's Samuel Johnson,
sharing the floor with Nietzsche,
Anthony Trollope, Franz Fanon, Osbert and Edith Sitwell,
German small-print dictionaries,
black-bound insurance tables,
histories of 1920 trolley companies that failed.
Even before you locate a book,
you can feel its weight
in your hands, the self-sufficiency
of 1870 geographies, the erotics
of steam engines. You're pushing the whole language
ahead of you, leaning your shoulder
into the cart and, when that doesn't work,
falling against it
till, just when you're certain that it won't budge,
it starts to roll as if it's considered the prospects
of staying in the same spot forever
and decided, instead,
to revel in the fact that it has wheels.
Hitler rides the same cart up with Marcus Aurelius,
Big Bill Haywood, the Marquis de Sade,
and Salvador Dali. Of course
you talk to yourself, but really it's more a hum,
the kind one keeps up

moving among bodies slumbering so deeply
they could be dead, music
that doesn't require the mouth to open,
as the mind sings to itself
day in and day out,
working alone,
on its way to words or on its way back.

O in Trouble

She'd have liked the young man better without the gun.
—"THE WHITE HERON"

One lucky classmate got Ginsberg, another Kerouac.
A third, Hemingway. I got a woman
with three names. A whole semester
with the spinster author of *The Country of the Pointed Firs?*
It was like being married to pudding, a diet
guaranteed to make a boy bloodthirsty.
I'd show the teacher,
dig up dirt, turn bobbins into dildos, a sewing kit
into a womb. *In her novels the women aren't just knitting;*
they are engaged in subliminal enactments
of penis envy. And that horse
on which the heroine rides? A huge vibrator.
Every reference to tongues or the deftness of fingers
privileges the reader to the coded subtext.
So, I said, as I pulled my essay out of the typewriter,
this was what it was like
to be a literary critic! What fun!

Got mad and stayed in my room. Bit my hand till it bled.
On the front page of her diary
the eleven-year-old Sarah Orne Jewett

drew both the *S* and the *J*
as serpents. *My monogram*
            with O in trouble.

༄ o ༄

Why did the very writer I was determined to despise
have to turn out to be not so different
from me? I was sixteen and chained to my genitals,
and had just learned to drink
myself sick. What hope was there for me
if I was going to fall in love
with everyone I read?

Lycidas

The ship having been damaged irreparably by a rock not
comprehended by the captain's navigational charts, young
Edward, instead of leaping overboard to save himself,
fell to his knees and began praying. Here we observe
an instance where one might have deferred one's pieties.
The drowning of this good man, nevertheless, prompted
a tome of hundreds of remarkably execrable poems.

—THE LIVES OF THE POETS

What's the point of being so pure
if you're going to end up celibate
at the bottom of the sea? Twenty-eight years of chastity
down the drain. *The dumb fishes*
swallowing into their entrails a man's tongue that had dripped
with the honey of his Greek.
If the poor boy had known such drivel would be written
at his death, maybe he'd have thought twice
and leaped overboard. Especially on a day so balmy
nothing ought to be allowed
to go wrong, the rock popping up
where no rock should have. It might as well have dropped
from the sky. *Dead ere his prime, Lycidas,*
and hath not left his peer. It was personal
for Milton, only a year older
than Edward King and still living
at home, mourning
the death of a very different young man.
Milton wanted language to rescue everything,

even a thoroughly drowned boy.

Saepius hic blandas sirantas sidera flammas

Ah quoties vidi superantia lumina gemmas.

Even the future author of *Areopagitica,*

the prissy young man

his classmates called the Lady of Christ's Church,

had a right to be horny

in Latin. In its walled garden

it was all right to hunger. Here he could

conjugate anything, talk freely

with the dead; they'd be luminous

in every spendthrift vowel, each extravagant

consonant. *Throats whiter than the Milky Way, stars*

that breathe alluring flames.

Scintillating?

Do you want to write like a sissy?
Even before he's through the door, he's taking off his jacket
as if that's all that tweed is good for:
being thrown onto a chair, though usually it falls
on the floor and he leaves it there to fend for itself.
Luminous? Pellucid?
He looks the class up and down,
the way you might a kid you're going to have to fight
eventually. Then he rolls up his sleeves.
Effervescent? All by itself
the adjective seems so naked, silly, sappy,
even the girl who wrote it has to laugh.
Rush to the defense and we're just as guilty.
Our teacher's going to root through our essays
the way Joe McCarthy did through the State Department,
get us to name names, turn state's evidence
on each other. *Transcendent?*
Exquisite? Blithesome?
Do the adjectives seek out the nouns,
lure them into their seedy embraces, lurid enchantments,
or do the nouns, on their own,
go looking for a little diversion?
Either way they end up contaminated,
flabby, effeminate,
even the toughest, most sensible, best intentioned nouns,

truth, beauty, justice.
What are they in the oily hands of the degenerate,
duplicitous adjective? What better place
than in the classroom
to stop America from going soft?

F this and *F that.*

One of the fringe benefits
              of turning sixteen:
       a boy can tell the whole world
to get fucked and fly
              down the street,
      as if his car were on fire
and the only way to put the fire out
            is driving
      as fast as he can.
O fuck for when he opens the letter
            that says exactly
      what he's afraid it would.
Go fuck yourself
            for when his father tries
      to persuade him
nothing will be different
            now that his mom's moving out.
      Motherfucker for the walls
that get in a boy's way
            in the hospital
      where his grandpop's dying.
Fuck. The teeth biting into
            the lower lip
      then the *ck*—just as good
as spitting into someone's face.
            Nothing else will do.
      Just when the boy's sure

he'll never be able to say what he feels,
                    this one syllable rises
          out of the great silence
all words inhabit
                    till they're spoken.
          Fucking A! It's the
kiss of a basketball
                    off the backboard.
          A key fitting
into a door he'd thought
                    locked forever.
          Light in a girl's just-washed hair.
Fucking A. Once again
                    words
          had not failed him.

Small *r*

For Israel Halpern

Who said letters had to go
  in a certain order
  like prisoners chained
together? The hard labor
  of the alphabet.
  Strikes. Insurrections.
Uprisings. Small *r*'s
  ripe to wreak havoc,
  free wheeling radical,
anarchist under cover,
  lurking in the heart
  of Parliament,
running rampant
  in the halls of Congress.
  The one of the twenty-six
letters you'd be wise not to
  rile, rib,
  ridicule,
relegate to the back
  of the bus. Wronged,
  r's reckless, rash,
relentless as rubber burning,
  a three-day rain, a
  robber on a bad day. The alphabet's

guerrilla warrior, propagandist
      grassroots organizer,
        r's armed and ready to
rush barricades, propel it-
      self up parapets. No valor,
        no gallantry, no virtue without
our runt, our rebel,
      each wall run against
        as if it'd never been
tried before, each rallying cry
      raised as if it was the first
        time it'd been shouted. Rabble-
rouser, revolutionary,
      r'll scratch and crawl, grip
        hold of air, if necessary,
erect its flag wherever
      it can. It refuses,
        right to the end, to
surrender. And even then it writes
      its own terms.

The CIA Tries to Dispose
of Still Another Mutilated Body

I collected martyrs the way a girl might collect movie stars.
There on page 242 of a book I kept quoting
just to make my teachers squirm
was the leader of the Congolese Liberation Party,
a man who'd been made to dine
on hair plucked from his own scalp
on the orders of the United States president.
Why had that former postal clerk been tortured
if not because he'd given himself to words,
their selfless martyrdom? Patrice Lumumba—
just to say his name was to fall in love again
with letter *l* and letter *m*,
to believe in the voodoo
of vowels. High-school English had been my first introduction
to imperialism; men in bow ties
who'd taught us that words weren't meant
to be used as much as whipped
into submission, hordes
of nouns and verbs, an unruly tribe with no purpose
but to serve their masters, a nation
of adjectives and adverbs held for centuries
in bondage. Ah, the tongue,
that wily subversive, mad dog,
relentless socialist.

"Memorize 'Dover Beach' for Monday"

As for rioting, the old Roman way of dealing with that is
always the right one: flog the rank and file and fling the
ring-leaders from Tarpeian Rock.

—MATTHEW ARNOLD,
"THE DUTY TO SUPPRESS"

Suppress this, I gestured
and slammed the classroom door, not just
on a bespectacled teacher desperate for tenure,
but on the entire nineteenth century's craven
imperialism. After all I was a high-school sophomore,
so there was no way I was going
        to think
about a fop with porkchop whiskers
who, intending to be conciliatory,
crossed out *crucify the slaves*
and, instead, wrote *flog the rank and file.*
Flog you! I shouted at Algernon Charles Swinburne
and Alfred Lord Tennyson.
        I didn't wish to learn
how Matthew Arnold stayed up all night
grading exams by the bedside
of his tubercular son. The author of *Culture and Anarchy*
romping with piglets
        in his garden?
Teaching his daughters figure eights
on the pond? The day before he died
leaping a fence

for the pure pleasure of being able to do so.
I wanted my enemies
to have the decency to be consistent:
                    pricks or prigs. Not to have
been fitted for leg irons as a child.
If I gave in and felt sorry for all the poets
who didn't know when to shut up,
let myself worry about the entire nineteenth century
and even the poor teachers who made us read
that panic disguised as elegy,
                    I'd not make it
to my next class, much less survive one more
day on this planet, its confused alarms,
its ignorant armies, its darkling plain.

A Very Short Sonnet Cycle

And so in nets of vanity lie taken.
                    —FULKE GREVILLE

I

Away with thee, self-loving lads
whom Cupid's arrow never glads.
So is this about masturbation? I remember
asking my tenth-grade teacher. The only way I could
tolerate sonnets was to turn them dirty.
All that posturing. Gripes, moans, sighs,
elaborate breaths expended, the higher algebra
of the conceits, the poet sweating over his beloved
like a chemistry experiment, turning her
into nothing but air, drawing her down
into his lungs, translating her
into blood and hoarding the beauty there.
All those labors to look easy, the deep sincerity
of their dissemblings, passion's contrivances.

2

Sir Philip Sydney, fatally wounded, called only for a sip
of claret, and then, before he could drink,
yielded the cup to a foot soldier, who,
as Sydney's biographer, Fulke Greville, put it, *had already*
eaten his last at the same feast. "Thy necessity
is greater than mine. Let it be that thy final taste
of the world be wine." A courtier true to the heroics

54

of the couplet, that commitment to dying
with grace, to suffering without seeming
to do so. Thus, when he fell it was the way light falls,
unquestioningly, as if slipping from one lover's arms
into the arms of another, light measured out
so elegantly, so iambically,
you never notice its going till it's gone.

3

The Lord Chamberlain was not on any tenth-grade curriculum,
but every afternoon our teacher opened his Fulke Greville,
a book so old we kept expecting its pages
to crumble under his touch, each boy sure
Mr. Fraser knew something about each one of us
that we didn't. *The end of flesh by reach of human wit.*
After being stabbed, Fulke Greville gave strict instructions
that his fleeing assailant not be pursued,
desiring that *Not any man should lose his life*
for me. I'd just begun to suspect what sonnets were
trying to teach me: it's not just what we've done
that matters, but how we speak of it
that proves our mettle. That's all
we'll be left, words, their hard choices.

Who Hears Talk Now of *Boudoir?*

For David Mook and Marsha Kroll

Or *Bidet,* our fading cinema queens with their bad teeth
and decaying furs? Or *Chantilly*
and *Crepes Suzette? Fortitude, Candor, Resolve*
as out of place as friars at a disco
or piano tuners on Mount Everest,
long-lost uncles, character actors
Dexterous and *Fidelity, Prominent*
and *Pre-eminent?* Cast in a play,
they'd be small-town bankers
who believed goodwill
would surely win out and then they'd fall in love
with the very women who'd make sure
it didn't, *Toilette* and *Soufflé,* with their thick accents
and expert hands. And what of *Lascivious*
and *Villanelle,* those old rakes
so deep in their cups, they couldn't get it up
if they wanted to? Pray tell
what news of *Sachet*
and *Locket* and *Linnet,* words so demure
you feel pure just saying them?
Poor old *Sonnet* still can't resist
longing for the one boy
in whom he's sure is distilled the very essence

of all beauty. And *Escutcheon?*
Will he ever forgive us?
And *Looseleaf?* Will she ever stop
writing angry notes
to herself and burying them among her lingerie?

Skinny Dipping

Once I found out that Melville had vacationed in Bermuda,
I began to resent him and his whale
less. It helped to know
that an author had other things on his mind besides writing
a novel so full of phantoms (over a hundred, I'd counted them!)
I couldn't help but lose myself in their maze.
What if Herman had met a real flesh and blood boy,
a kid who showed him sights
off-limits to most tourists, coves
so secret the two of them had no choice but to
strip and swim in waters so blue
even the author of *Moby Dick* couldn't cast enough of a shadow
to darken them. His Nore Mutiny book refused
to let itself be written. He was still grieving
over his son's suicide. Perhaps
he mistook the surprising affections of a civil servant's son
for the world's attempt
at some small act of recompense,
an informal apology. I could understand a boy being so lonely
it seemed a privilege
to call a man by his first name,
to be of use to someone old enough to be his father,
so in need of comforting, the only way
the boy knew to help was to take off his clothes
and lie down under him.
Maybe Melville made a garland of hibiscus
for the boy's neck, rubbed flowers

into the boy's skin so
when the great poet made love to him
the boy would smell of angel's trumpets and gardenias.
Of course no one has ever heard of the kid.
Who keeps a record
of every time that light finds a man's face
or an unlikely breeze cools his brow?
There's no room in a biography
for every bit of shade a genius has taken refuge in,
all the birds that woke him up,
every furtive embrace. Or perhaps
some parts of our lives prove
too important to trust to paper,
too difficult for words.

Biographical Fallacy

526 pages on Brook Farm, the over-soul, and Ralph Waldo Emerson?
A few of us laughed out loud.
A few cited *cruel and unnecessary punishment.*
It was like being caught out in a hailstorm
with no shelter in sight. Several vowed revenge,
held the teacher responsible
not just for one lousy hour, five days a week,
but for everything wrong in their lives.

At home I'd read a few pages and then look out the window
at a whole armada of hills hoisting anchor.
How was I going to survive an entire book
on Transcendentalism? You can only masturbate so long,
but I squeezed as much out of me as I could
onto Henry David Thoreau, smeared Melville,
let a few drops fall on Louisa May Alcott.
Maybe I'd have paid attention to the text

if the teacher had told us that, after reading a report
on the House Un-American Activities Committee,

Matthiessen had opened his window and walked straight into the night
air that seemed to expect him
and did nothing to break his three-story fall.
I was seventeen. Despair I understood.
Words and their hopeless crushes, shipboard romances.
It was 1958. No one talked of the anguish of men

who called each other *Devil Darling*
and *Dear Rat*, *Pictor* and *Piccolo*.
The biographical fallacy, a crime invented at mid-century
by English teachers to shame
other English teachers. If only I'd known
to take a book as seemingly endless as the sky and sit with it
by my window and try to puzzle it out
the way I tried to make sense of the stars.

Maybe it'd have taught me what the stars couldn't,
what I am still trying to learn today.

The Pathetic Fallacy

For Pam and Herb Perkins-Frederick

His bedroom was filled with gallon jugs
of urine he wouldn't let any of his visitors throw away,
a sort of maze we, his students, had to pass through
to get to him. Was he still testing us, bottle
by bottle, a gallant troop, a private army, his palace guards?
Nearly blind with most of his heart
man-made, two cancers under his belt,
he had suffered so much that we'd forgotten
how each illness required new courage
of this sweet grammarian who had tutored us with such devotion
that we had often confused him
with the language he'd tried to improve
in us. There are plenty of elegies for young
drowned men, but how many for the prematurely
old surrounding themselves with bottles of urine
as though they now expected
a conflagration so terrible they'd have to
rely on their own body's fluids
to put it out, gallon after gallon, their last defense?

The Saint Meets His Match, The Saint Goes Underground,
Pope's translation of *The Aeneid,*
The Collected Trollope, the last five issues of *Baseball Digest,*

a whole library of French semanticists
piled on the hospital bed,
on the bed table. If he was going to be attached
to machines, tubes running into all kinds of places
on him, he refused to suffer
alone. He brought Sir Philip Sydney for company,
Samuel Daniel, Edmund Waller,
and the entire sixteenth century.
Coleridge shared his bed along with Flannery O'Connor
and John Woolman. If he ever was going to indulge himself,
what better time? Piled on the bureau:
The Lysistra, The Inferno (in three translations), *Paradise Lost,*
and *The Life and Death of Buddy Holly,*
books heaped so high
it looked as if he was conducting an experiment
to test precisely how long before everything collapses.

⥤ o ⥢

Dead?
> *Dead!*
Why any of you could be dead,
pipes a bird cheerily
as if no other morning existed but this,
no other branch but this very one.

Listen, *that bird knows Elizabethan poetry better*
than most of us. No, I'm serious.
Who else hooked up to an IV,
surrounded by young men who adore him,
would be arguing the merits of the pathetic fallacy?
You flatter me too much,
blushes the rose. *O how you do go on!*
insist those little hypocrites, the daffodils.

☙ 0 ❧

At nineteen to be allowed to call my professor
Bob! To fold his wheelchair
into the back of my car, see that he got where he needed to go,
and pretend that only I could get him there!
Once he clutched at his chest
and I thought that he was having another heart attack,
but he was only grasping for one of those notebooks
he'd go nowhere without,
like a lung he carried in his breast pocket,
his way of breathing in
Molière, Goethe, Thucydides, Gershwin,
Conway Twitty, Sister Sledge, Richie Ashburn, Dr. J.,
Fulke Greville, the Marx brothers,
a miniature blueprint for a medieval castle,

malapropisms from student essays,
a few calculus problems still to work out,
all in a brown spiral notebook. He even had one in his robe
at hospice. Dying was not going to stop him
from writing down everything
he was determined never to forget.

Don't argue with me. I did see Jesus,
Fraser said it with such conviction that it was hard to remember
that here was the same person who had trouble
buying a pair of shoes. He absolutely believed
in the music of the spheres, the genius
of doo-wop, and the transfiguration of Christ,
and tried to persuade each of us
as if offering a gift he was so excited about
he'd started unwrapping it himself. *This is it,* he'd say
to a kid with blue hair sitting on his bed,
and he'd turn up the small tape recorder he'd taken everywhere,
Follow the tenor. Notice how he starts as backup
and then takes over the song,
how the lead singer defers to him.
He's got the voice of someone who's drowned
and been brought back to life. You're right,

it is another language at first. Okay, this is the only decent song
on the album. But it is really good.
It is extraordinary. There is nothing quite like it.

How is the professor doing? we'd ask.
Now that he was dying, we'd stopped calling him
Bob, except when we were helping him
to the john. It hurt him even to piss. He had to think hard
to move muscles he shouldn't have had to worry about.
And so he dragged his wounded body closer
and closer to the ledge, and then, one morning,
shut his eyes and let himself fall.

The cords of death encompassed me.
The torrents of perdition assailed me.
The cords of Sheol entangled me.
The snares of death confronted me.
In my distress I called upon the Lord.

The trees clustered like a family of mourners
who'd not be consoled. After the service
we walked in the sunlit garden,
wiping our foreheads, complaining of the heat
because we had to talk about something. Each of us had to
look somewhere, so I chose to stare
at the flowers, the way the wind made quiet inquiries of the grass
and the way the grass answered
demurely, the branches trembling
faintly as if someone who'd passed there
had brushed them aside. Was it a ghost?
No, only another breeze
eavesdropping, a merry
impish, lilac-petaled breeze lingering
to hear what a man will think up to praise it.

∽ 3 ∾

abecedarian n.s.   *The word is used by Wood in his Athenae Oxonienses, where mentioning Farnaby the critic, he relates that, in some part of his life, he was reduced to follow the trade of an abecedarian by his misfortunes.*

—SAMUEL JOHNSON,
THE DICTIONARY

The Burden of Being the First Letter in the Alphabet

For George Drew and Jim Freeman

A's responsible for the whole
                    platoon. Awake,
          it takes the first watch.
Absolute allegiance required
                    of this combat-
          weary vowel.
At ease? The most *A*'s
                    allowed to relax
          is to stand. At alert.
At parade rest. What if it fell
                    asleep at its post?
          All of Western civilization, all
America depends on it, the entire
                    English language.
          A go on furlough?
Ask for a little R & R?
                    Take a nap?
          A coffee break?
Agitate for better working conditions?
                    Adequate compensation?
          A vacation? Maybe the whole
alphabet's due a raise.
                    A work stoppage.
          Strike! Unionize!

Agitate! Each and every one
                    on the assembly line.
              At last, time off from the
Arduous labor asked of
                    all twenty-six letters
              and which they do
And have done and will do again.
                    And again.
              And always for that
Abysmally low pay.

Boycott Lettuce! Boycott Grapes!

Give my four-year-old a word
beginning with *b* and he's a baby again,
blowing bubbles from
his own spit, taking small
bites of air—
Boycott, boycott!—
bounding up to shoppers,
barking like a puppy
who won't take no
for an answer.
Boycott! The store manager,
rushing out,
can't help but look
bad, shouting at a little kid
who hands him a leaflet
the way a dog might drop a
ball at the feet of someone
either too stupid
or too lazy to throw it
back. My son's grown
more accomplished than
any puppy at
begging. All day he coaxes raisins
or cheerios out of my pocket.
This is his job once I

begin feeling sorry for myself:

        to make me chase him

    chasing leaflets blown

between cars. *125% higher*

        infant mortality.

    800,000 children

below the ages of 16. Maybe

        a picket line's not the safest place

    for a child. *Boycott!*

Boycott! The first grown-up

        song my boy's learned

    by heart, words and their

brazen politics,

        and he won't, at supper,

    not even at

bedtime, *maybe never,* he

        boasts, stop

    singing them.

The Vanity of Human Wishes

Baby Maggie's cooing in the doctor's office
is so exuberant, it's hard not to imagine
she's talking at last
to the world, apparently having forgiven it
and us for the two shots in her leg
        just minutes ago.
My oldest boy's started speaking to me
again, describing in detail, down to the wide rim M452 tires,
the car I ought to buy him
when he turns sixteen.
        And for the first time
since war was declared
no one's left a message on my answering machine,
threatening to kill me, though I don't stop worrying
about my student in the reserves
who loves World War II movies and popcorn
and at 6' 10" can't help being a walking target
        in the desert.
The only bad news I hear
from the nursing home is that my mother forgets sometimes
and goes to stand and falls in front of her wheelchair
and looks up at the nurses
as if it still surprises her
        that her legs won't work.
I've just paid off the mortgage
and, for some reason I can't fathom,

the car doesn't need as many
repairs as I thought it did.
                    And it's my friend's anniversary,
nine weeks to the day off drugs,
and he's celebrating the only way he can
in jail: smiling at everyone,
                    even the guards.
The light rushes to meet me
as if it's been waiting for me outside the prison gates
                    all day,
and I can't believe how lucky
I am. Nothing's gone wrong,
nothing promises to go wrong, and I don't know how long
I'll be able to go on living
                    like this.

Trying to Make Sense of a Single Word

For five days my father-in-law has been doing his best
to die, his eyes shut tight
as if he's decided that it's the only logical thing to do,
though he hasn't convinced his lungs.
They keep working hard
the way you do in a business just about to go under.
My wife and I get to the hospital before the early morning shift
as if this is our first really important job
and we're determined to prove we can do it.
It takes a few days before we can eat
in the presence of someone who can't
taste food anymore. Because we don't know what else to do,
we go on talking to Keesta,
making ourselves useful,
pretending that he's squeezing our hands back.
Not till her father dies
will my wife realize that she's knitted a blanket
big enough for two families,
will I discover I've written the same people
twice. We hold an old man's fingers
to our lips as if to speak
directly to them. But they go on conversing
with the air, teaching the light what it always needs
to be reminded of: it's meant to do more
than fall. These hands know something only the dying do
and can't or aren't about to tell us
what we must learn on our own.

True Readings

*Everything's built on water. No matter what grand
architecture one erects, one keeps coming back to the
same dark canals.*

—THE LIVES OF THE POETS

What bad luck to finish the definitive
edition of Manlius's *Astronomica* at the very moment
the world stopped being interested
in Latin and Greek, distinguishing between faithful translations
and true readings. In Venice
the Cambridge don, Housman—in England so fastidious
he'd not let even Wittgenstein use his toilet—
kept an account book with the occupation
of each boy he'd picked up—dancer, waiter, gondolier
—and how much the boy had cost.
Out of penance? Pride?
Or pure amazement, each foreign tryst
a riddle, that, if studied, might finally make sense?
Of course it was flattering,
the distinguished professor brooding over the boy's belly
as if the lad were one more sacred document
scholars had spent centuries trying to
decipher, stroking the boy's shoulders
as if he'd been carved out of the light
and water of Venice and the poet
couldn't believe it possible
anything human could be that cool to the touch.

Soon the boy would prove not to be a statue
by putting his penis in the professor's mouth so that afterwards
the professor would put money in the boy's pocket.
A boy's got expenses, even if he looks like marble
that the rain's rubbed smooth.
Housman may have been the world's most respected
authority on Propertius, but that didn't keep him
from trying to read the vulgar Latin
of a boy's flesh and succumbing to the fate
of the language that he so revered,
its doomed polysyllabics. *Dissolution. Disintegrations.*
Momentous and grand. Rome toppling.

The Importance of Punctuation

My darling, death calls me, and there is no way, I fear,
to resist. Please, forgive me, but . . . ,

It is hard to imagine my father writing that note,
and not putting in every comma,

to fail to do so for the editor of the *Harvard Business Review*
a greater disgrace than wandering, naked,

through his hotel and then, after being led back to his room,
swallowing enough booze and pills

to kill a man. *Such unrelenting a pain,*
it is like an arrow, one lodged deep in my heart,

too deep to pluck out, any other way.
The commas go on fussing about, unflagging servants,

doing, once again, what's asked of them,
old valets trying to prove that they're useful, still,

that their master cannot live, poor fool,
without them. *An arrow, dearest, I can't, no matter how I try,*

pull out. I keep coming back to the commas,
what my father loved about language,

that everything counted, the smallest words, the dark,
diminutive curves that drop below a line,

even writing a suicide note,
my father taking care to observe the niceties

of punctuation, to honor, if nothing else, the rights
of words, to let each have its turn,

saying what it must, *Please, beloved,*
remember that no matter what my hands have done,

my heart continued steadfast, to the end,
your faithful, your devoted,

Not for Love or Money. Not on Your Life

—with thanks to Betsy Sholl

No, said the cabbie when I asked him to change the station.
No, said the waiter when I tried to apologize for spilling the soup.
No, said my mother, when I begged her to stop firing her nurses.
No, said my daughter, when I told her she'd feel better tomorrow.
Not now. Not ever. On no account.
Under no circumstances.
Oh *n*, what we would do
without your almost blissfully stubborn
negativity, your fervent
refusal to look
on the bright side, your delight
in slamming the door with such emphasis
it'll never be opened again? Doctrinaire. Single-minded.
Devoted to your convictions.
The nail driven in:
Nada. Null. Nicht. Nein. Nope. Nah.
As if that's what the mouth was made for:
to find fault with as much as it can,
to settle for nothing
and to relish doing so.
Unn-uunh.
No sirree.
Not on your life. Not now.
Never.

The Dropped Stapler
Just Misses the Baby's Head

Just married, other things on my mind, I *almost*
stepped off the platform
into water rushing right over Niagara Falls.
That'd have made the honeymoon memorable
for my wife! A few years later,
carrying dolly, diaper bag, stroller, baby, and briefcase,
I got distracted and *almost*
threw my son in the trunk and strapped last night's work
in the car seat. Another time,
late for the movies, I took a wrong turn
and *almost* wiped out my car full of kids.
Even the most well-adjusted
would have trouble living with that: *almost*
locking a toddler up with a tire iron,
or obliterating a whole family
on the way to *Pinochio.* If it weren't for *almost*
I'd be on the side of the road
staring at a dead dog. I'd be at my sister's grave,
telling her how sorry I was for not hearing the ring
when she was one phone call away
from killing herself. *Almost,*
you may have rescued us more times
than we'd like to admit, but there's a cost
you exact. It doesn't matter
that I did pick up the phone,

that I swerved in time,
that I didn't drop the ball in sixth grade
and lose us the championship,
that I didn't spit in my boss's face,
that I didn't take the rest of the pills,
that I didn't slap my son as I was about to.
I could have. I might have.
I almost did. *Almost,*
you're going to make us pay
one way or another.

It's Not the End of the World

He slumps to the floor, sobbing
as if even his tears are too great a burden
for his three-year-old body to bear. But when I try
to pick him up, his arms flail, his legs kick out.
I might as well try to gather a burning bush,
or try to reason with
flames. If he stops wriggling, then he'll have given up all hope
of getting back the key chain
with its hoop of keys, light, and a whistle
his grandfather gave him.
No matter that the whistle has been broken
for weeks, the light had grown so dim
only he could see it. For days he kept taking out the key chain
to see if it was still there.
And now it isn't and it's your fault,
Daddy, Momma, Opa, Floor, Crack in the Pavement;
how could you let this boy lose the very thing he needed
to close his fingers around
right now? So what if the keys fit no lock
in the house? If he kept trying door
after door, finally one would
have the good sense to open. It's not the end
of the world, we say. His father, grandfather, mother, favorite aunt.
But we're wrong. Only a few moments ago
the world had been as good as it gets:
a key chain in his hands and six keys

he knew individually
the way a blind person knows the faces
of everyone he loves. Now where is the whistle
whose hiss he'd come to count on, its familiar cry
of alarm, the pleasure of blowing air
through any hollow place? Where is the little light
he used to flash off and on
till it became a language only he and his bedroom walls knew?
The world's taken back what it so generously,
so unexpectedly, gave him.
So what choice does he see now
but to lash out at its most impressive representatives?
He's not about to forgive his dad, life,
or the entire universe for the way things fall
so determinedly from his hands.

No Extenuating Circumstances

Phil's here because he drove his car straight
into his father-in-law's place of business. Bobby's locked up
because he couldn't keep his hands off his wife's
baby sister. Artie held a gun
on a stranger and made her drive till he got tired
of thinking what to do. What if there was a test
to identify who's going to be a carnapper
or crackhead, who's bound to
knock off armored cars or push down old ladies?
Then we could extricate them from the third grade and not waste
their teachers' time or party hats
and cake at birthday parties
they shouldn't have been invited to. Expel them
from peewee football. Extradite them from Sunday school.
Excrete them from junior high. Why
wait till grade school? You want to get rid of crime?
Start early: extirpate certain dangerous babies, x them
off the planet. Get rid of that chromosome
before it's got a chance to
sell drugs to your children or pick your pocket.
Every safecracker with colic.
Every dope fiend before he's weaned from his mother's
breast. Look at X. How his legs are spread,
his feet planted as if he expected
to be caught, thrust against a wall,
arms stretched out, palms flat,
with no excuses, no explanations, no ex-

temporizing. This is what X wants to know:
what good is language if it can't help you
figure out the very things
you most want to? A quick exit?
Exile? X doesn't have that luxury,
all he's done wrong, all he'll have to pay for
on his shoulders now,
past and future.
There's nothing else to do but hold up the world,
keep it all from crashing down.

Count to a Thousand
before You Open the Door

*Hope N. 1. A person or a thing on which one may base
some hope, 2. A feeling that what is wanted will happen.
Akin to G hoffen Orig. Sense (?) to leap up in expectation.*
> —WEBSTER'S NEW
> WORLD DICTIONARY

Even as the breath's being let out
   for the *h,*
the throat's narrowing
    to the *o,* that zero
in disguise. *Just like a girl,*
   her mother had scolded.
Making things up,
    begging for attention.
Her brother had, once more,
   locked her in the closet
and tried to push his body
    into every opening
in her till even he got scared.
   She was nine. *Better not*
tell your father,
   her mother had warned.
Hope. The *p*'s soft explosion.
   The silent *e* once again
knowing more than it's saying.
   In the waiting room

the young woman hunches over
                as if shoved down
into the seat. Warned
                years ago
not to move, she's still
                obeying.
Though the light insists on falling
                on her hands,
her face, she's still counting
                in the dark. *Inhale.*
Exhale. Swallow. If only she could
                scream, even now,
shout, sob, turn her breath
                into something more
meaningful, more
                merciful than air.

Maybe

Maybe it's time for you to go,
        suggests the manager in a voice so level
it's obviously an order. He's staring
at a man he should never have hired
        in the first place.

Maybe, now you'll listen to us,
say the children whose father just set fire
to the kitchen, cooking supper
for his dead wife. Now you'll let us find some place
safe for you.
        Maybe, answers the father.

Maybe you could step aside,
        repeats the cop.

Maybe, says the elderly woman as she stands in the road,
        arms folded,
while the first of the trucks starts toward her.
It's got a power plant to build, more
important things to do than jam on its brakes.

Maybe you'd be good enough to stop
screaming,
            says the man
as he clamps one hand over the woman's mouth

while the other fumbles with her zipper.
Perhaps this isn't such a good idea,
maybe it's not too late to let her go and run.

Maybe I'll get out of this alive,
thinks the woman.
                    Maybe I won't.

No ifs, ands, buts, or maybes,
a friend pounds her fist on the table.
Dump the flowers in the trash
and start packing before he gets home with more
promises.
                    Perhaps, the woman says.
Possibly.

It's what the child says to the ice
as he steps onto it.
It's what the ice says as it creaks under his boots.

Perchance, says the wind as it tears into the trees,
                    this time
I'll let you off with a warning.

Maybe, the heroin pleads,
it'll be different this time.
Maybe, the blood says as it makes its deliveries.

Insufficient, Incompetent, Incapable

You don't need a mother
or father to drive you
insane. There are prefixes
already willing to indict
impugn, and impoverish
you. Indelicate, Inquisitive,
Intrusive,
that team of Viennese-
trained psychiatrists, take notes
of everything you say
and don't
say. The Infectious, Infested,
and Inflamed
Insurance Company's
only too eager to stamp your claim
invalid. Invidious,
Insidious, and Insubstantial's
prosperous Main Line law partnership's
entire practice is devoted
to proving you're not
not innocent. You're implicated
even before
you open your mouth,
impeached long before you take office.
The more you try to prove
that you're not an imposter,
not irrelevant, not insignificant,

the more you are.

What mercies you've begged

from language, that harried bureaucracy

of suffixes and prefixes.

Irreplaceable,

incomparable, indispensable.

Ah to be just that,

if only for

one intoxicated, intimate, infinite,

highly impractical,

improbable, and incandescent

instant.

Here

Here—always lives—in the Now.
—EMILY DICKINSON

Here you go, Maggie says
handing me the half-crushed Cheerio she's spotted on the rug.
She's just discovered the secret pleasures
of the adverb. *Here,* she says
as she offers me a cotton ball that felt so good
in her mouth that she wants me to taste it too.
She can't get over this new privilege
granted her: being able to stand on her own two feet
and pick things off the floor,
a sliver of glass, a dead fly's wings,
bending down for them making them all the more valuable.
Here, she says, as she nests a yellow cup
inside a blue cup. She can spend a whole morning
making sure red still fits
into purple as if she already knows
that nothing in the universe is predictable.
It's got be tested over and over.
Here's the cat just where she thought that she left it.
Here are tiny ships sailing through the air
someone will eventually explain are dust motes.
Here's your father! At day care
sometimes Maggie will look up the way very old people do:
as if they can't quite place the face

of the person they know must love them.
If she's hard at work erecting towers that she fully intends
to topple in the next few moments,
teaching herself the difference between *now* and *then*,
Maggie will pay no attention to whoever has come
for her. It wouldn't be fair
to abandon blocks that hadn't had a chance yet
to get used to her hand, to leave this deserving *here* for a more
problematic *there. Here you go,*
her daddy says, as he lifts her into the car seat.
Here, that single syllable that's half location, half longing.
The first consonant can't help sighing,
though the second rides in to rescue as it so often does.
And the two *e's?*
They do what they've been doing for centuries,
servants so quiet that we don't even notice they are there.
Here I go, Maggie says, as she's buckled in,
as she looks out the window
to see what the world has in store
for her, here and now.

My Son's First Real Attempt to Grow a Beard

Now that he's sixteen, my son's tired
of urging paint out of tubes and forcing it
onto canvas, cajoling cadmium,
pleading with alizarin, bullying vermilion,
demanding Persian blue, cobalt, umber, and azure do more
than they seem willing to. He demands burnt sienna
show him something he's never seen before.
So he goes into what he calls his studio
though really it's just our garage
and turns on the video camera and grimaces
and grins and remolds his face into shapes
you'd expect that it'd take if gravity gave up all pretense
of keeping things in place. At first
the whiskers seem to have no intentions of growing
just to please the camera,
and yet two weeks later, there my son is
with what appear to be spines, so many it almost hurts
to look at him, the way it does staring
at cactus. As a boy I loved the time-lapse films
of the desert blooming, petals unfolding, nature
speeded up. I wanted beauty
to happen right away. And here I am now
a fifty-year-old man with a son who spends his days
mugging before a camera in his garage
and calling what thorns its way out of his dark follicles
art. It started just a year ago

when his body decided to take its blank canvas
and improvise: a light stubble on his chin,
a few straggling hairs under his arm, a whole meadow
that'd begun to sprout
in his groin, and then one day I looked down
and black threads were growing
out of his feet, his hair even more menacing
when he started shaving it off
his skull. A fifteen-year-old with a five o'clock shadow
all over his head? His first attempt
at postmodernism. *What's the matter
with paint?* I want to ask now.
*Why can't you just fill up canvas with flowers and clouds
as you used to?* Here's a picture of him
sitting in front of the camera at 9:04 Thursday morning.
Here's a picture of him sitting in front of the camera
at 8:57 Friday morning.
What's the point of all this? I ask.
Exactly, my son says
and strokes his chin and lets his gaze drift out the window
where the light's doing what it did yesterday,
what it will do, we hope, tomorrow.

"The business of a poet"

said Imlac, "is to examine not the individual, but the species;
to remark general proprieties and large appearances:
he does not number the streaks of the tulip
or describe the different shades in the verdure of the forest,"

wrote the author of *Rasselas,* who'd visit on a typical day:

with Boyse, who, having sold his clothes for paper,
wrote, naked in bed, reaching through the holes in his blanket
to scribble one more ode to a mouse;

or Dr. Levett, whose entire medical credentials were
that he'd been a waiter at a Parisian café where doctors drank aperitifs;

or the widow Porter with her rouge
and spoonfuls of laudanum and so many affectations
talking to her was like eating cake
that was nothing but frosting;

or the cat Hodge of whom the author of the dictionary said,
"Why he's not the best cat I ever had,"
but then added, stroking the cat's chin,
the very place it most preferred, "But he's a very fine cat, indeed."

Or Sir Joshua Reynolds or Sir David Garrick
or Pol Carmichael, the *reformed* prostitute;

or Psalmanazar, who, knowing no one in England
had ever been to Formosa, including himself,
made up a language to teach the young missionaries
whom the archbishop was sending to that distant land
where, Pslamanazar said, flowers grew
in sand and silver could be scraped off the surface of its lakes;

or every other rake or scoundrel, pedant or poet
who'd sit in the alehouse and let the old teacher who'd scolded Milton
and taken Donne and Shakespeare to task
talk till he was tired enough to go home;
this cantankerous Idler whose terrors weighed more
than the Dictionary and who spoke as if each sentence
were entrusted with the task
of not just keeping England glorious, but the earth
spinning and the dark
from having its inevitable sway.

❦ 4 ❧

I am not yet so lost in lexicography, as to forget that words are "the daughters of earth, and that things are the sons of heaven." Language is only the instrument of science, and words are but the signs of ideas: I wish, however, that the instrument might be less apt to decay, and that signs might be permanent, like the things which they denote.

SAMUEL JOHNSON,
"THE PREFACE TO
THE DICTIONARY"

What If You Could Be Any Letter?

The world was all before them, where to choose
Their place of rest and providence their guide:
They hand in hand with wandering steps and slow
Through Eden took their solitary way.

—PARADISE LOST, BOOK XII

Once again my students in jail look at me as if I'm crazy,
but they do what I ask. It just so happens,
they remind me, that they aren't going anywhere
for the next 4–6 years. I've worn down their ringleader
till he's finally willing to be a little silly. From here on
even the warden will have to address Jason as *S*,
as, he says, in *sly, slick, stealth*. Once I've got him on my side
the rest join in. *S*'s buddy, Carlo,
is *T*, the bodybuilder, the muscleman.
Eric, the one the rest call Mouse,
lingers over the letter *R*
because his grandmother used to call him Little Ricky
till he'd been arrested so many times even she gave up on him.

Eugene decides to be silent *e*, not a bad choice
for a pickpocket. Pete and Roberto got busted twice
together. They're always quarreling,
inseparable even in jail, so we nickname them the dynamic duo,
Q and *U*. The smash-and-grabber, Daniel, is *D*
because he doesn't have much imagination,
a fact which explains why he keeps getting caught.
We get into an argument over C. *It's K*

in disguise, says Eliot, the stockbroker
serving 3–5 for supplementing his income
by selling cocaine. *It's cagey. It's crafty.*
A cutthroat. A conniver. It's coldblooded.
It's chaos. It's catastrophe.

Most of the men gathered at the table
are here because they heard the ladies might be allowed
to come to this class, but now
that they're stuck with me, we get down to work.
At least here they get college credit for engaging in fantasy.
Today I want them to pretend that the planet is doomed
and there's just one spaceship
and they've got to choose who lives and who doesn't.
(It beats mopping floors or dishing out potatoes.)

The world was always coming to an end
when I was a kid, and there was no time to talk
about anything else. *A meteor is heading for Earth,*
I'd say to the boy that my mother had made me play with
because she was friends with his mother.
We've got the last rocket, There's not enough room
for your whole family. Pick someone.
We'd spend the afternoon deciding
whom and what we'd save, which books to take.
That was one of the rules.
We had to lug language on board.

Imagine that we're drifting in space.
What do we do to pass the time?
I now ask Tiny, the three-hundred-pound check forger,
and Moon, the second-story man,
and Steve M., the shoplifter, and Steve R., the carjacker,
and Phil who fell asleep in the house he was robbing.
Tomorrow I'll get one man remembering
the aunt who taught him to cook,
another, the long year his father wouldn't speak to him.
I sit with a third, and together we try
to recall snow falling on water
or what rain really tastes like.
For a few minutes we decide to pretend
this is the real purpose of life:

floating away not just from the prison
but the planet and looking back at the earth
from our space station, giving up
on the mother ship ever remembering to return for us.
We've got no supplies,
just this intrepid crew. *A, B, C, D, E, F, G, H, I, J, K,*
L, M, N, O, P, Q, R, S, T, U, V, W,
X, Y, Z, the first inhabitants of Arcadia,
now homesick, curious exiles from Eden,
navigating their valiant path through the universe,
always looking back
over their shoulders at Paradise.

Say the Magic Word

Cottage cheese? Special noodles?

No, thank you.

Juice in your favorite cup?

No, thank you.

Toast cut into soldiers?

No, thank you

To be not quite two and free

to say *no* all day

and add *thank you,*

so gracious,

so endearingly reasonable,

no one has the heart

to argue with you. Pears and chicken?

No, thank you!

Sweet potatoes and ham?

No thank you!

Till you must wonder if this large person

who talks like a used-car salesman

is slow-witted. And then there it is,

exactly

what you wanted: macaroni

and cheese

and the man you call Opa—

because you like the *o*

floating in the air till the *p*

gets impatient

to be spoken and the *a*'s a question
                    waiting for its answer
—blows on the macaroni
                    and you blow too. It's fun
to do what Opa does, so easy
                    to get him laughing,
that must be one of your purposes
                    in this life. His is
to drop everything and run
                    when you say his name.
What a life this is! More milk
                    than you can drink,
a blanket that smells of sleep,
                    everyone ready to tell you
what a good job you did
                    in your diapers,
rub cream on your bottom, and let you
                    sprinkle powder
on the cat, and apparently
                    this will go on
forever and ever, it seems
                    world
without end.

No Weapons of Mass Destruction Found

Of course the newspapers are angry at being lied to.
The press, the investigating committee,
the appropriate government officials,
everyone expresses dismay except for, not surprisingly,
my granddaughter, who is too busy
chasing the cat, and my nine-month-old grandson,
who has his own problems, because
every time his sister bumps into him or the sun
gets in his eyes or he tires of a toy
he cries. I don't need a network of intelligence agents
to know what's wrong. All I have to do is search inside Tyler's mouth
where the two subversive teeth, those little terrorists,
are wreaking havoc in his gums,
and so I dance him from the last place
he felt awful to the next place he hasn't had a chance yet to fill
with his sobs. I hum louder
than his crying, as if to make clear to the pain
that it's met its match in me.
Later I peel what's soiled off Tyler
and Josie and plop them both in the bath
and ask the water once more for a miracle,
and then I bundle them in towels they immediately throw off
as if that that's the whole point of taking a bath:
running naked afterwards through the house,
intending never to dress,
pretending that one's free to stay like this forever

if one wishes, the object of everyone's
scolding, everyone's delight. For now
there's no point in turning on the television or radio,
no call for any news
but this. *For now.* These two
three-lettered words may be some of the most important
in our language. For now.

. . . *y*

For Lynn Levin

may look jaunty, as if it hadn't a care
                    in the world,
          but consider what it must
carry on its bony shoulders, all the heavy
                    artillery. *Anxiety.*
          Worry. Jealousy.
Responsibility. Beauty. Integrity.
                    Duty.
          Loyalty. Is that why
y can't resist making *tomfoolery*
                    out of *tom,*
          presto-majesto, *monk* into
monkey. Y's the waiter balancing a tray
                    who seeks out
          the one spot that's wet and
dizzily, defiantly trips
                    and spills it all. *Flummery.*
          Frippery.
Flippancy. It's almost as if *y* wants
                    to make English pay
          for yanking it from its native
country and turning it psychotic, psycho-
                    somatic, psyche-
          delic. *Sloppy.*

Silly. Dopey. Want to discredit something?
Simply add
y and you don't have to
worry. The guy who stands
at the corner and talks
to his hands? *Crazy. Daffy.*
Loony. The woman who opens her arms
to anyone kind enough
to sleep with her?
Slutty. Sleezy. Scummy.
Voyeur, voyager,
cynical old Greek,
maybe it's not the floor that's tipsy,
maybe the world's just too
slippery for anyone to stay
steady for long. For every miss
a mystery.

Zero: A Found Poem

with thanks to the OED

1

The lowest point or degree; vanishing point; nothing, nullity. Also an absence or lack of anything. Informal: one having no influence or importance; of no worth. A nothing. A nobody.

2

In mathematics, a variable or value for which the function vanishes. In grammar, the absence of an overt mark, written or spoken, as against its presence in corresponding positions elsewhere. The grammatical zero has all the rights and liabilities of the thing it replaces.

3

Zero-able. That which may be omitted from a sentence without loss of meaning.

4

In the theory of games, applied to a game when the sum of the winnings of all the players is always zero, one person's gains matched by another's losses.

5

Hawthorne: "In the zero atmosphere of America."

6

To zero in. To adjust the aim or sight by repeated firings.

7

The iron tablet marking the position of Tyburn-gate is virtually a mile-stone, identifying as it does a spot from where the miles on the two great roads that join at the Marble Arch are measured. It is perhaps the sole survivor of all the zero marks of London.

8

Zero grazing. Zero growth. Zero tillage. Zero tolerance. Ground zero.

9

Zero. Initial point of a process or reckoning. Absolute beginning.

10

Carlyle: "Unless my Algebra deceive me, Unity itself divided by Zero, will give Infinity."

11

Neil Armstrong: "In zero-gravity, no matter how little or much we ate, we were always full."

Babbadino

Babbadino, me babbadino,
Zack says, his mouth pressed to my ear
as if he's not going to trust the air
to carry the words he's just learned:
Babbadino me. You can't go to a store with Zack
and not come back without something that bounces
and has stars on it. An earth with air inside it.
A wiffle ball. A Nerf ball. A super ball
that can be squeezed inside a two-year-old's palm
and yet can hurdle whole buildings.
God knew what he was doing when He invented
rubber. What more could one ask for
than something squishy, that jumps out of your hands and hops
down the sidewalk as if it has some place important
to go and it's your job to follow it. *Zack:*
a fist of consonants, capital Z marching out to meet all
who dare approach. *Zack:*
a kid who'll forge his own destiny;
a catcher who'll work his way up from the minors;
a tough negotiator who'll settle age-old conflicts
between warring states; a congressman
known for his principles. Right now Zack's too busy
to worry about the future
his father's picked out for him. He's marveling
at the miracle of roundness
we call a ball and he calls a *babbadino.*

Some kids are like that, you've got to scoop them up,
bounce them on your knee,
then put them back on the floor. You treat them
with the same respect and affection
you would a ball. Zack's blissfully intent
on the rubbery thing rolling in and out of his hands.
Babbadino! Zack will shout into my ear
as if *ball* is not a round enough word
for something that caroms
off walls, windows, ceilings, something so marvelous
it could roll and roll
forever. It's not going to let anything get in its way.

Walking the Beach, September 10, 2001

I like seashells, Jake announces as he holds up periwinkle
after periwinkle, as if each one's so different
it can't be left where it is. *I like periwinkles,*
he says, the way kids do
when they've just learned a word and won't keep
from the pleasure of saying it again
and again. *I like limpets. I like mussels. I like barnacles.*
I like razor clams. I like spoon shells.
Is there nothing on the beach this kid doesn't like?
He can't just pick up a shell,
he's got to declare his degree of commitment to it,
as if, at three and a half, he knows that it's not enough
to fall in love; you've got to make the world
understand just how much.
I like canoe shells, Opa, but the big, spirally ones too.
And the ones with ripples. And this one
with scribble on it. Jake greets each day
as someone might welcome a long-lost cousin
who's crossed thousands of miles
to meet him. If these shells had the patience
to travel such great distance to get here and were willing to be
broken in the effort, then he sees it as his and his Opa's job
to gather them all. But it's exhausting
liking so many things: shells the color of old dentures,
clams even the seagulls tired of, the ruined armor
of horseshoe crabs. Jake throws himself into his work.

Life would so much easier for him
if he didn't need to see, touch, know everything,
feel that it is all up to him
to make sense of the universe. The world can't help
but disappoint this child. Finally
it will have to break the heart of a boy determined
to pick up every snagged fishing line, washed-in buoy,
every tar-stained dog whelk, heel of a slipper shell,
ponderous ark, spotted moon.
Jake's got a whole beach to cover
and only so much time.

The Sixth Letter,
the One with its Arms Outstretched

Fear was my father.
Father Fear.

—THEODORE ROETHKE,
THE LOST SON

Tell the fifteen-year-old
that at sixty he'll still be crouching over words
in a room grown dark
around him, muttering to the squiggles, dots,
and lines he's just made on a blank sheet
because sometimes it's not enough
to put a word down on paper, he's got to feel it
in his mouth and he still can't
fathom how letters decide to fit together
to make *father* or *final*, so much asked of a single, fatigued fricative like *f*:
to fling us forward to our fates.

Tell a fifteen-year-old
he's going to find himself just as frightened
at sixty as he was at five and just as fascinated
by the shape of a letter,
that he'll still be scribbling his thoughts on pages
no one will ever see, still be just as dependent
on a few obliging vowels,
a few more recalcitrant consonants to make the future
bearable, give a little dignity

to failure, allow him to whisper a word
over and over
as if he was telling *l* and *o* and *n* and *e* and *l* and *y*
a secret only they could understand,

and now he has a name
for what he has felt
for six decades—21,950 days!
He writes the two syllables down: *Forlorn.*
O *f* and *o* and *r* and *l* and *n,*
dear romantics, my sweet consumptives.
There'll come a time when you'll have to make do
without me. But for now you're mine.

What's Worth Keeping

For Bill Wunder and Camille Norvaisas

Finally even the winds find themselves bored
with picking through the rubble
and turning up nothing worth keeping.
Whole buildings sprawl on the ground
as if they've thrown themselves there
like men who, grown tired of years of standing
upright, make up their minds
right then, on the street, to crumble
and stay that way forever,
the one choice that can't be stripped from anyone:
to collapse, buckle under, give up.
People wander the streets because they don't know
how to live if they aren't expected somewhere
or don't have anything important
to do. Right now
it's breathing. Right now it's making some sort of sound
they can still bear hearing
rise from their lips, words that make sense
when a girder is lifted off
a crumpled child or as they sift through ashes for a missing
brother. This rocking back and forth.
This wailing kept up till it has a life of its own,
until it could almost be a song.
The mouth once more daring the lungs

to deny it this basic right, daring the air
not to fill with what's flung into it: shrieks, lamentations, curses,
the mind and body still working together
even if they can't make sense
of what has happened,
making sounds in the throat, singing to a world
even if the world can't sing back.

What's Missing in the Dictionary

What did Webster know of the sound
             of sand packed around you,
of being nothing but a head
             on a beach? The way your feet revel
in mud, the delicious pleasure
             of getting stuck and unstuck?
Even the OED. has no term
             for snow under your collar
or the sting of soda bubbles
             up your nose. Not even a phrase
for what rain smells like
             before it falls
or what got you through the day
             your grandfather died.
What's the Latin for the stretching
             of time after a boy's best friend
leaves for camp, or the compressing
             of a whole childhood
into one dive into trees
             reflected in a pond,
those rapturous seconds
             when a girl breaks surface
and knows that she can do this again
             and again? There ought to be
a better word for what a kid does
             alone with his body.

How about *Ooolalala*

        or *About time?*

What does Webster's have to say

        about wiping your father's

buttocks, or holding your son as he flails

        in the water? Or watching your lover

lose his hair, or a friend get the award

        you'd hoped to win,

or a bird peck at the hard ground

        as if it owes him something

and he isn't going to stop till

        he's got what's his?

The Visitor

Sent to Hell, Sir, and punished everlastingly.

On the morning before Dr. Johnson died,
a stranger, a near-blind girl, pushed into his bedroom.
Even before his friends suspected
that she'd opened the front door, she had
lifted the small, troubled congregation of his huge fingers
and held them to her face and demanded
the great man bless her. Only a week before,
the author of *The Vanity of Human Wishes*
had urged the physician's hand
to stab deeper, lancing the swollen leg.
Later, he had found scissors and driven them into his calf.
To go to the root of the infection?
To cut away all that was vile in him?
I will not be conquered. I will not capitulate.
Now barely able to shape his breath
into sounds, he—already convinced
of his own irredeemable wickedness—
did bless the child as if he had decided to believe
words still had a right
to do that: not heal but make tolerable;
not lighten the load, but enable one
to take up its heavy weight; not restore sight,
but help one bear not seeing.